Writer
Bartender
Skateboarder

Poems
by
Ryan Marcel Buynak

Writer Bartender Skateboarder

Published by Coyote Blood Press
& Paradisiac Publishing.

www.coyoteblood.blogspot.com

www.paradisiacpublishing.com

Killer Cover Art by Ariel Wilson
Links: www.arielwilson.com

ISBN: 1717290876

Coyote Blood
will cut your heart in half…

Life is a funny sunset.

I wish my mom would've had enough money
to let me take guitar lessons.

But then we probably wouldn't be here,
would we?

Poetry Sucks

Your lipstick was a forklift,
my youth is past's shadow.

None of this is true,
and none of it matters.

However, where we go reflects
where we've been and the things
we've seen, the things we've loved
and the people we've left.

When I was a kid,
I hated reading and writing,
but things change,
and some things stay the same,
especially coming of age.

I didn't choose poetry;
It chose me.

Mix CD, Summer, 1996
(Orlando, FL)

1. *Harry Bridges* by **Rancid**
2. *Bullion* by **Millencolin**
3. *Linoleum* by **NOFX**
4. *It's What You Do With It* by **Pennywise**
5. *Disconnected* by **Face to Face**

Poem

I poured her a heavy glass of Gruner
and watched her sink sad on the other side
of the bar.

I could tell she was beating herself up
for falling in love
with a dumb poet bartender.

I consoled her with silence
and wet wrists.

I did a bump in the bathroom
and when I came out she was gone.

Poem

Never thought of the future.
Always creative.
Writing songs without being able to play.
I liked words and want,
but didn't know what to do with either,
until…

Poem

Skateboarding is not a sport.

it is an art form.

Those Quick Breaks in Young Days

I would come home from school,
and eat a snack
while watching Comedy Central,
before going to work
at Arby's or Office Max or Disney
Or Tony Roma's.

It is in those quick breaks of the day,
that I discovered my love for comedy
via Tom Rhodes, Mitch Hedberg and others,
but Rhodes happened to be
from my home town,
and that gave me hope.

That one day I would be bigger
than my youth,
defined by something
other than being a high school dunce
and a bad busboy.

#Pancakesforthetable

of suede and sugar,
won't you dance the way you dance
and ice skate for me?
I am addicted to your unfortunate laughter.

I just poked myself
in my owned eye
with my bandana
that usually resides in my back left pocket.

then I crossed my heart and hoped to die.
there are pictures on the wall,
and everything I do reminds me of you.
spell your name, cast me backwards, listen
to the loud werds that I write.

great legs,
you make me want to be a lifeguard.
you make me want to build a playground
and then burn it down.

enjoy the crocheting
because life and love never take holidays.
I am the saltwater gypsy,
and life is for living.

in a city of lately rain,
not all of us are wanted,
yet with some weird
and wayward divination,
some of us are lucky enough
to speak of revolution.

Bathtub

I want to write a poem
and call it *Bathtub*.

I just want to get in it
and take it for granted.

oak fake.
palm of hand fate.
the pressure and misspellings.

pineapple soda gal.
no more gin up the stairs.
no more summer.

wrinkled fingers,
on real, working, writing arms.

for fuck's sake.

Coffee & Tea & Whiskey

I was the champion
of a one-man band,
but now I am a folding.

nickels and dimes
be me
or be mine
while
moments are time
and vice versa.

I have laid down
in the arms of absence,
opened up my eyes
in existence…
over lattes
and Earl Greys.

put whiskey wishes
in between my teeth
and knuckles.

The only thing
you ever loved
is passing your heart.

5th Street?

come hang tonight, come burn,
so says Franco in his internet voice,
which sounds like murder to me,
yet I listen to his mouth math.

sure, we always combine for good
punchlines
on Wednesday machines
on Earth.

but we are, indeed, state of the art
when not lazy and selfish,
and when not scared.

from other days called younger brothers,
like the records we have owned,
or ordered,
and traded or broke,
or given away to fine gone girls.

unlike our model friend,
we would never do this:
run. nowadays.

fun is somewhere,
probably found under fossils

of dinosaur hair,
begging to be lifted up,
and discovered.

woke up like this

I am in a feisty mood today
and I don't know why.
I yelled at a woman this morning
about how her Christian beliefs are bullshit
and hypocritical.

She spit on my shoe.
needless to say, this did not
make the morning better.
Plus, the bagel place on 89th and 3rd was
packed.

I am not hungover.
I am not at a loss.
I am not Mercutio.
Just some days see me tempered and
roused.

It is not because of a her.
It is not because of lonesomeness.
It is not the weather.
Some days you are allowed to awake in a
shitty mood.

I wish my high school guidance counselor

told me that this is okay.
I wish sister told me that this (probably)
happens to everyone.
I know it happens to Chris Corso.

My lonely Friday adventures
will not be boring, at least.
Maybe I will eat cupcakes for dinner.
and watch Back to the Future, because that
always makes me feel better.

I Love Tennis

I played varsity tennis all four years of high
school...

it is in my marrow,
but I wish I played more.

I also wish that I could
work the US Open
each year
in Queens
with my friend Daniel.

I picture us setting up the event
with barricades and bullshit,
bartending and flirting
with rich, old white ladies.

maybe, I will sign up next year
and try to get Daniel to do the same,
if for nothing but the stories.

Whenever the Waves Smell Weird

beautiful girls
are like storms
that leave you wondering.

I am watching an old show
called 30 Rock.
My friend Marc
worked on this show.

these facts,
these ghosts
make me feel old.

I would rather leave
something to sweet lonesomeness,
than invest in lounge act love
again, especially considering.

SK8

I used to bring my skateboard everywhere.
now it hangs in a closet.
but I still see stairs and wonder.
can I 180 them?

This Is What I Did Today

Said Hello.
Towards no one.
Killed a bug.
Sprained my ankle.
Killed the way of the wonder.

Got full.

I haven't scene.
all that can be seen.
Slappy Sundays.
Astor Place, of course.

ever heard crickets.
not my sad soundtrack.

drank wine with Kahlua.
passed the time.
because that's all I had.

My songs were happy, immense.
Weighted. Waiting.
My feet were made for the sea of concrete.
My heart was made to be poetic.
My hands were made to be chopped off.

Poem

Hey, Eric.
Do you remember that time
we meat Keanu Reeves
at Biddy's?
The three of us drank beers
and talked about Point Break.
Keanu bought blow,
and then we went back
to my place.
He didn't even do any of the yak.
He kept washing his face
in my kitchen and bathroom,
but refused a towel,
just letting the water
drip onto his shirt
and my floor.
Marc is still mad
he wasn't there.

Skateboarding in Flip-Flops

When the existential crisis comes,
I pull a rock to fakie,
and keep going up and down
on the mini ramp,
despite my 21-love,
and my fractured wrist.

The oohs and ahhhs
of the crowd,
all friends and foes,
have my balance,
as I force my heart to manual,
throwing a beer into the fence bushes
while I surprise myself
with my balance.

Speaking of Red Wine
and Tan Lines

You will be happy on some sad street
that wishes to be a bitch of a beach,
washed with hand-me-down towels,
tongue-tied too tired…

Are you going out of town?

Let's go to the show
after aloe.

I am trying to quit
after just one sip
of Merlot from the toe.

Let's be forever
for just one night,
or our one thousand moments
don't have to die.

You gave me crabs
and unpaid bar tabs,
so don't be overly dramatic,
because you will be happy
one day

when you are willing
to be.

New holes in old clothes;
it's the soothing fit
behind the general admission line,
where cigarettes and time
catch up to us
in a gathered kiss;
this is it.

Ignore patience.

Werd Up!

I love my life
 here.

on
 Earth.

Her?

Cater Waiters

this
February 26th.
From noon to ten.
PM to PM.
20 dollars an hour.
Plus tips.
Must have Tux.
And be able to sell your soul to the devil.
Over *hors d'oeuvres*.

Needed.
Money, too.

Write later.

do you ever have ham dreams?

I sure do.
skateboard ham dreams
with sandwiches
and silly suicides.

I got pepper stuck in my teeth
and salt down the front of my pants.
I need a haircut.

if you see me with a rifle,
don't ask what it's for.

in one misspelled werd, what's on your
mind?

Sk8ing.
Forgetting.

Hospitable

I bartended forever.
From fifteen to 30 (hopefully not 50).
I can't forget the nightmares I had.
yet I enjoy the regrets.

But time is like sand stuck in a guitar.
It will rattle until that guitar is given away.
Or set on fire by a better musician.

A steady girl,
terrorized
and found.

me,
I am a monster\
 Growing,
  hopefully.

When I was young,
my eyes were hazel,
now they are brown.

WWYFSD?
(What would your favorite skater do?)

Blast like Cardiel would.
Balance like Daewon.
Boss like The Boss.
Stick around like Markovich.
Scream like Getz.
Travel like Kenny Reed.
Stick it smooth like Supa.
Rep like Rodney Torres!
Turn it into art like The Gonz.
Be Bobby Puleo.
Shit like Sheffey.
Get gold like Guy.
Shoot and read like Rowley.
Coast and kill like Koston.
Invent like Way.
Make like Hawk.
Photograph like the Temple.
Invent like Mullen.

Go be a skateboarder.

Poem

rain, rain,
don't go away,
come keep the peace
between these sheets.

her bluegrass eyes
keep closing.

truth be
dead friends,
dead cellular telephones,
dead nights,
resurrected midnights of tomorrows.

I Am The Greatest Thing You've Ever Seen

never counted on a road quite like this.
want to cut my head off and throw it up in
the air.

I wrote this poem on a paper bag inside a
dream.

I'll measure it against today.
hairline fracture, don't give in.
poets are sluts.
motorcycles washed up in floods.
long the way unknown.
some die young.
some get old.
simple.

rope on a soap road.
harness the cheese before winter again.
winter again makes me laugh.
I pick my boogers after work.

I sing.
satisfied.

I live on and on and in.
life is a funny sunset, in-fucking-deed.
in the name of truth.
I will someday die in a doorway.
if my yesterday is a disgrace,
tell me you still whisper my name.

98 Moore Street, Brooklyn, Tomorrow

I hope this is the first clue
to the raddest scavenger hunt
in the history of the world...

or just the address to a really
great pizza place.

try me for free.
I wanna be your sick music.
that of the Hipster Generation.
this is what it's like to be a human wolf
robot.

so many spaces
in between our places
in time
if it exists.

every body knows
how this jingle goes.
sung from thin sunny lips.
you found my cigarettes.

I curse the setting

and eventually fall asleep
on the rumbling subway.

win with me, red cup.
yeah me wild while I dream.

recognize me, tree of knees.
I made no sound in cypress.
I will borrow straight back to you, blues.

Poem

I like touching oceans.

The Recipe
(for *Buynak Chili Biscuits*)

first,
you gotta be poor
with the motivation of a stoner,
 but with more gusto,
or the anticipation of hunger.

then go to the grocery store.

the store on the left corner
is better for this dish than
 the store on the right corner:
you only have to buy four things.

chili.
my lady's a vegetarian,
so I grab Amy's Organic shit.

mac-n-cheese.
I prefer Velveeta Shells and Cheese.
These two things can very in brand name
and shape,
but the biscuits are goddamn important.

because they aren't biscuits at all!
stay with me here, trust me.

purchase Pepperidge Farm Texas Toast,
because it is the symphony in this situation.

also beer.
doesn't matter what kind really,
as long as it is not a hefeweizen or some
kind of hazy Double IPA.

this dish is best suited for the cold months,
so open up a window,
and turn on some music.

Music recommendations:
 Avett Brothers or The Head and The Heart.

open the chili and pour it
and one beer into a sauce pan and
put that shit on the stove on a good low
simmer.

preheat the over and pop those "biscuits" in
for eleven or twelve minutes.

poke yourself in the eye
on accident.
sometime in the middle there,
you're gonna wanna bring a pot of water to a

boil, and get the mac-n-cheese in there,
ready, easy.

the end result, the horizon, the film-setting
 is a big bowl.

put the fluffy bits in first.
then cover one side with chili,
and the other with mac-n-cheese.

then look at it,
 sit back,
drink another beer,
and enjoy.

you can thank me later.

your taste buds might murder you.

Home or Heaven

you're on the few good sides of leaving.
I'm on the bad side of coming back.

prairie dog, porcupine, cup-leaver,
this dust bowl is gonna be awesome.

from the knees of *needs-it-this-time*,
I scratch at the painfully playful earth.

pay attention to the porch
and who's coming down the stairs.

please,
no materials.
no
thank on that.

goddamn it,
sometimes life is so good.
then what?

it might rain tonight.
petrichor, who gives a shit.
night is a lovely blind girl
from the south.

Fakie 50-50, Shove-it Out

The ledge was just right.
And I was in love.
Just high enough.

I will eventually be murdered by this city.

that she eats rattle snakes

poetry reading
went west
and terrible
tonight.

with solar.

self-fulfilled prophecy
in the middle of a weak week,
unproductive at best.

sick at worst.

lucky to be dead.
embarassed to be alive.
Thursdays taste like cars and exhaust.

unprotected sex.

favorite four-letter word: *hope*.
I am not a five-letter word: *shark*.

I hope life forgives me.
my fangs are reluctant.
my heart is fragile.

In Technicolor

never been to Governor's Island
before…

it's not what I expected.

neither is the
New York City Poetry Festival.

met the Denim Skin,
The Great Weather.

unknowingly consumed
some weed brownies,
miraculously sweated in the rain:
I thought only California sweats in the rain.

I was recognized once or twice or three
times
by other bastard poets without saints
who know my work
from a two-years-ago time lapse:
the poetry treachery, skate punks,
and the Brooklyn dykes.

I am not the same poet I was back then.

I am not the same person I was a moment
ago...
I am black
and white
these
damn days.

she said she was coming today
but I didn't sea her.

The city looks good from here
this gay ferry
fishing the east
with me of the upper beast.

I used to be better at adventures;
now I am just a part of them.

If There's Time to Lean, There's Time to Clean (Arby's & Voodoo)

it's weird getting old.
people start dying.
even distant memories.

my friend Justin's
dad passed the other day,
and I've been thinking about him.

he would give me food
when I would pick Justin up
for school my senior year.

and every damn day
that song Voodoo by Godsmack
would play at the same time.

Chris and I worked for him
at Arby's while we were in high school,
and needless to say, we were lazy,
dumb, laughing kids.

I'll never forget,
he always said to us,

that if there was time to lean,
there was time to clean.

at the time,
I thought the man made that saying up
and I thought it was so clever.

I haven't seen him in years,
and I am sorry for my pal,
because getting older sucks.
and losing your dad is the worst.

skateboarding in the brooklyn cold

I am leaving tomorrow.
so today I drain in the rain.

remember when we were.
in Tompkins Square Park.
and you fell on my skateboard?
that is an adorable memory.

I cross the street.
Minnesota, here I cum.
looking forward to midwestern gals.

ollie up the curb.
hit a pebble and bust my ass.
remembered I am not 13 or 23 anymore.

my flight tomorrow is early.
so I go collect my belongings.
and drink myself to sleep.
in the ruined celebration of life.
on the outskirts.

maybe I will bring my skateboard.
and never come back.

CAPS-LOCKED LUNATICS

we prey for language.
we laugh like horny cartoon characters.
shaped like wolves or colorful coyotes.
and we write manifestos every single
fucking day.
five lines in our stanzas.

while we dance on pages.
also skateboarding and drinking beer.
throwing darts and pulling sharks.
as well as wishing over drawbridges.
while stealing the stars.

this is what it is like.
in our community.
two bullets, ten *as-we-speaks*.
guns and weeks.
gone but not gone but gone but not gone.

no edit has us by the spanish balls.
no end can mean it all.
the typer is wilder than both of us.
we just have to give it the gas and the drugs
and the universe;
the stuff.

we will not be parentheticals.
we will be forever.
grinded into iron.
burned into some sort of stone.
called *The*.

Bullshit

the gusts of wind
start up,
shoot in,
sounding like
a marching army.

outside,
in the danger,
leaves let me down.
I went outside to taste the weather.
the twigs told the story.

I walked to the river,
and walked back,
waiting for rain,
or to witness a cow flying by,
mooing.

I only saw some midnight robin birds
milling about like hollow-boned criminals.

inside,
laid,
out of the blue,
the microwave gives one long beep.

I unplug it.
it beeps again,
this time longer.

I proceed to walk five blocks to the river,
with the microwave in hand, still beeping at
random,
in this bullshit storm.

everything moves,
everything pulses,
everything lies in the eyes of the eves of
you.

I chuck the microwave into the river,
and count conspiracies on both hands.

The rain starts and the army of wind
marches around the corner.

The Setting

dessert in the desert.
Montreal.
West Hollywood.
Portland.
Taipei.
Louisville.
love.
Seville.
broken wrist.
Berlin.
Chicago.
breakfast for dinner.
Tel Aviv.
Harlem.
candles everywhere.
Denver.
Seattle.
Witchita.
Sao Paolo.
Orlando.
Seattle.
Prague.
midnight mornings.
cigarettes again.
it's over.

On and On and On

on her way to the door,
she turned back,
and said "I hope you live a long time."

baby steps to my right,
I moved,
stabbed out my cigarette
on the low brick wall.

I'm getting by on one meal a day,
catching the crayons in a paper cup.

"Thank you," I say.

Shut + Rot

No more losing war(s),
let's do so many things wrong,
caroling.

while walking and getting lost
late at night on an empty street
on an empty stomach.

I have never done a damn thing right,
doctors say don't have this much blood,
because I am a surgeon
in an old fashion way,
and I will cut you.

with love.

Lolly

Never could have imagined.

Otherwise

Other people are wiser than me,
singing sadder songs.

It all
makes me feel so wrong and healthy and
right
at the same time.

I'm just a kid.
Praying and preying rent to a divorced sister.
Love keeps passing me by.

Other than that.
Other than wise.
Be less.
I'll be less.
Than I.

Than Eye.

My face in the ground.
I am messing around.
With happlings.
All of the time.

I guess I needed to open up and let it all out.

There's gonna be some one-liners in this shit.

And this is an example.

The Girl with the Key

I'm in love
with a gorgeous woman
that still sends letters.

She wears my rings,
and says great things
into my good ear
at suppertime.

The Kansas Silo

I want to write something called
the Kansas Silo,
while I am at work
in New York
or Montreal
or Somewhere trying to forget
and move on.

the stars couldn't be brighter.

Kansas, I want to believe you,
and I want you to believe in me.

Poem: I Will Eat You

cons are there.
joy is a funny fading sunset.
built for bastards without saints.

take my hand
and help me forget to understand.

Ms. Tonight

I made a list this morning and you are on it.

I'm so full of courage
and shit,
 but I don't know where to be.

forever.

make a movie and sweep you off your feet.
Mine.
I'll be back from Portland in the fall.

life is full of full circles.

Years are mean.

Poem: I Am An Eel

I'm from Florida.
originally.
free greed and blisters.
get silly.
forget the rest of the past.
grass.

But New York made me.

I Miss My Friend

it takes a few glasses for it to settle down,
life grey.

beacon of *bigbadnewswolfdeath* hangs
from my collar.
and I still have to go to fuckin' work.

the world is weird today.
one less friend.
and subsequently, I am helplessly angry
at the world,
but what's the use?
time is stupid and silly.
and the timing of left turns are
sometimes widow serious.
I am the jack-o-lantern's sad, wayward
smile.
the heart is on the menu for Tuesday's
breakfast.

Eat my heart.

with a side of horrible-things-to-wake-up-to.

I find myself staring at the shelf

with a thousand boxes of grief in my arms,
and I need some help
carrying them downstairs.

(I want to send a letter to all my
GoodFellas and tell them that I love
them.)

rain and snow are appropriate on
such a day,
the day I fell in love.

He was the toughest dude I ever knew.
I can't touch his middle name
but I wish I could.

I Stop

You stop,
the only sitcom
is mine.

I stop,
the only semicolon
is yours.

Better Than Brooklyn

I've lost a lot, too, dear.
How's your morning?

Clouds and cancer can't kill us.
Silent thunder.
This feeling is from feelings long ago.

I was in Brooklyn last evening.
I was in Portland last summer.

Skateboarding on ice and regrets.
Keep your hands where I can see them.

The pride of staple days.
Be mine, be better (than Brooklyn) and
yourself.

Her Arms Work

her arms work
like beautiful miracles
under microscopes
while I shake martinis.

cut my thumb
on disaster
and said too much
twenty town minutes
are different than city scum shots.

Held Hands

I read terminated papers.

And.

I can barely get to sleep.

A Honda Civic for a car.

Life in a jar.

Ten years in ten sleeps.

Dreams about a hole in my face.

I stored stolen scissors there.

I know you think.
I am some kind of fool.
I can be lonely.

If.

you are happy.

After all.

Stupid Toast Today

Run me my fever
and tell me it was worth it
to honor the tradition
of this great companionship
of beer and poetry...

Like televisions on fire
on the first Thursday
of every month.

It is a signal fire,
goddamn it,
to muses.

I don't blame you
or burn you.

My hands may hold you.

Forever in
these pages with
which witches say Have Singing Edges.

Undone,
like a sweater from Long Island.

Forgotten,
like a river treated like water…
How did it get this way with words?

The Rumbler rumbles
under New York City,
and I tumble along
and I have found a way to celebrate.

A snake eating its tail:
the eternal return
living loud upon loud.
Unapologetic,
fore fire be,
writing for free,
ultimately.

This is a Song called This is a Song

my match burns
in the background
with parallel peaches
and pineapples
and peacocks
and a tomahawk
and a hammer
hiding above the city.

Elm Street, Montreal

Let's move here.

Babe.
There.

the one with the blue roof.
and the tiny bench in the front yard
the one on which you sat and looked so
beautiful.

Folksy

spoke to Everett on the telephone,
while listening to the sparrow and the wolf.
his little brother is back in jail.

what are you doing Thursday?
are you free?
Everett, unlike his brother,
is free,
but trapped in Florida.

I have a poetry gig in Oakdale,
at some college.
colleges pay big.
gonna take the train
and get drunk in Long Island
on the way.
Wanna talk?

standing tall isn't easy,
I say,
looking down isn't hard.

Sell all your furniture and stay warm,
he says,
buy a cottage near the sea.

I assure the world
that real wars
happen in silence,
in cottage doorways.

the weather is nice today
here.
how is the weather
there?

use your eyes for everything
except love.
follow your heart for everything
except life.
and false alarms.

I wear these jeans because they were on sale
last year,
and I speak because I can.

Spoke to Everett on the telephone
while listening to A Darker Shade of Blue.
Apple Lewis is dead at the neck.

heroes die, too.

Slept on the moon
and wrote fiction.

don't drink until the devil turns to dust.
Didn't think until this.

two-thousand years,
we will still be here.

Poem

I just realized I am wearing
the Fleet Foxes shirt
that you Somewhere got me.

no need for further police intervention.
I will disappear.

this is not how it is supposed to end,
but
I will always love you.

have lion with jumper cable lips

in the first place I made my heart
with electrics and cause,
I dug a hole with cattle bones
and buried the day,
grief and all.
the sunset winked at me
and I killed the lights.

in the first morning,
answers were in the garden,
my knees were cold yet running old,
where I discovered the day
had grown
from a seed
into a window.

I went and found another lover
in the window point of view
where I saw you
with tiger.

trucker be damned,
knees and please,
come catch me.

raincoat

writing poetry is easy
especially
when living is hard.

Five Out of Six

five
dirty
wives
live in between a preacher,
shut the door and rot in hell.

Holy Toledo!

we will be ruined
soon,
my love.

clever as the moon.

I like my teeth.
I want to keep them.
forever.

do flies ever go to sleep?

I hate when I overhear people at the bar
bitching about having to come into the city.
stay in Brooklyn then!

and, dear General,
it is harvest time.
Sacrifice.

I want to live in an old abandoned
schoolhouse.

I hate then when people write
C'est la vie.

walk on my back.
I stand by the dishwasher,
thinking of the window,
thinking this is the way.

Hashem, this is the one.
We will will.
Our way.

I'm not sure.

I hate when people say
this last year I have been mostly
focusing on work.

...on the floor of the ceiling.

the Rumbler is filled with
reggae tonight.

I am not a tiger.

According

Wisconsin, Atlanta,
I pray for the past.
Kansas, Long Island,
I pray it will last.

I'm happy in my way,
reading books on the train.
The four or the dicey five,
still alive.

It's a good thing that I was your neck.

vulture soliloquy

I skip across the busy street,
head of attic architecture
and the future mouth
of this.

all of this.

just a bartender with a dream;
just a poet and a bankrobber.

I am a man of my werd,
and that werd is *Unreliable*.
and probably misspelled.

Only bad things happen in Brooklyn.

this is redemption
under a blanket.

vengeance under the man-made sun.

trust.

I don't know what to call it.

sf

doorbells.
airplanes.
bridges.
music.

are we alone?

no.

limitless with these connections.
all on our ground.
in our sounds.

bugs at night.
midnights at midnight.
dust.

all of it.
and us in the middle of it all.

get up in them guts.

The Trapper-Poet

I read about death,
but I don't live about it.
tigers of the heart,
hyenas of the mind,
coyotes lapping at the limbs.
Of both three easy beasts
and easy men,
this is 86th street.

An Affront to the Exalted Silence

It is winter finest
and made for the eyes alone.
Play for rain lately
and the city town we live in.

Los Angeles, A.D.

I am writing a book about
this bastard place.
It took my heart in 2004,
but gave me a soul in 2005.

From Venice to Silver Lake,
I was lost and looking,
yet this place let me ride
its subway searching for cocaine.

With a skateboarding vision
and a Hank Chinaski dream,
I thought this place would be different,
with different girls and goals.

I will never be famous,
Especially on the back of broken poetry,
but at least I will be painless
because of trying.

The Throat of a Coward

The sound of a coward, too…

The lice of a coward,
itching.

Needs and needles.
Needles and old.
Needless to say the cold.

I am scared of the Devil
showing up in my throat again.
And affecting what I say
to the all-over audience.

Kill myself with natural death.
Kill myself with heart break attacks.
And the facts,
And the zoos.

I have stole from people
Who have stole from those.

You were young.

Once.

Porcupine

Your chin will grow
with the barn that leans backwards
with lies.

Forty dollars
and cops
on Morgan Ave.

I'm going to LA
and then Montreal
and then Berlin
and I will get over you over and over again.

Less than,
Marty is somewhere there
and he says he has a plan,
despite Avery and his stupid whore.

This will be LA for good or ill,
and everyday is a weekend.

I was the runner
who could only give her less/
when we exist,
we lie.

I used to drink a lot of Mad Dog 20/20
in middle school,
celebrating the hands of losers
and the World Series.

I hope you are sad.
I hope you are so fucking sad.

Yeah.

A Refuge of Last Resort from the Darkness in their Own Hands

I would be a tale
Unfold.

Each day,
The barman
Required.

Sterling, my stoop
with piss of agony and daily,
that which was once read
with love
and
the exampled turmoil
of minds
that have caught up to regret no matter what
for those things lost.

What is the train saying?

The boots upon the floor.

By girl by smoke rolling alone,
yellow all, drink,
write this.

Through Pains of Sugar

I was with Crazy Leslie
and Everett last evening,
and we all pretend to keep the nights.

And Vernon was lost,
and Garfield was a monster.

I told him over and over
That I won't go to Brooklyn ever again.

We were drinking fermented orange juice
spiked with orange juice and whiskey
on Country Luke's roof.

He was about to turn into Country Mick.

Then out of the fucking blue
Country Fuck puts on a song
and I remember strange hands
taking my wrists again…

And peaches and pineapples and peacocks.

I am a burglar.
I steal the night.

kingsofar

I'm not well
from wishing.

over draw bridges.

or at 11:11.

on the goddamn LIRR.
Lindenhurst no more.
no one reads this shit anyway.

I pronounce it oddly,
with a weird accent, she'd say,
a mix of Florida and somewhere else.

this is a different train.
and a different train of thought.
wobbling, this is all that I have.

plus the fresh air in my lungs,
the lint and the lighter in my pocket,
and the coins in my hand.

what a buzz to be me.
I think mirrors are funny friends,

like television sets
and other living rooms.

I wish I had the guts to scream.
Things are exactly what they seem.

Not *not* party to a mess,
Neverknowing can kill you.

We Are Sending a Postcard
to the Mountains

in the tired thick thistle,
in the doubt of the city,
do I have a night owl?

hold my hand
as we run from bandits
with saxophones instead of rifles.

let us detail the turn-away
and don't let birthday water
fall on a Friday.

For Short Years

We were breaking news,
lost inside the wind,
trapped in each other's necks,
all the while,
witnessing our own respective resurrections.

We were waiting,
but never waited.

We tried,
but we were too afraid to really try.

It was real,
but all too real.

puke this song

Corso and I feed hamsters to coyotes.
of course.
then throw rocks at trains.

I get drunk.
He eats leftovers.
voicemails and missed calls.
life goes on.

and we celebrate things.
things we make.
like mistakes.
like pottery, poetry, and decisions.

Paper Plates

I piss in the wind
out of balcony sin;
it's dark in this backyard alley
aside from lights of other kitchens'
windows.

Or other windows' kitchens.

I open a grocery bag
with a knife
and a little bit of miracle spite,
tossing a hundred and ninety paper plates.

Giant paper snowflakes

Let's pretend
into the gusts,
they all float up to heaven's gallows
and towards the river to the east
with little notes written on them.

Halloween Hurricane

Adroit.
Cake.
Mystery, what's west?
Eye whiskey.
And coke.
Cola.
Northeaster.

Baseball facc.
October is almost over.
Of union square.
I hope a haunting bench gets blown away.

Some dude had a seizure.
On the J train.
Yesterday.
Around 6:44.
I transferred trains.
Conscience?
No.
I use dictionaries.

It's not raining.
That much.
But the wind sounds spooky.

I have a hundred boxes.
Somewhere.

Open-Faced Baked Black Bean Sandwich

Jalapeño baked black beans
on a hearty yet soft seven grain bread
with a silly toss of sharp cheese
topped with a perfect fried egg.

Knife Time

we were down there w/ the scum of
the earth.
easy.
east of way down there.
The Standard Biergarten.

I am antler face.
and this is my birthday water.
she is knife time.
and we make a big difference.
as life distracts us.

Your Cousin Gary Doesn't Believe in Dreams
(Co-Written by Josh Mendelow)

Cousin Gary, an expert
in "Modern Mayan History"
does not believe in dreams...

 not aspirations,
but the kind of dreams you have at night,
says he has never had one.

So why would you invite Gary to the game?

The Knicks know he is here
and they will lose,
all because of his massive indifference.

Gary is not an asshole.
He is just a schlub.

When he introduces himself
he sorta shrugs like he is somehow
apologizing (for existing).

Your Cousin Gary is a weirdo.

He eats onions like apples.

When he washes his hair, he only uses
conditioner.

Gary only has a Discover card.
He cuts his own hair.
He's really into trains.
He is lobbying to bring back the Seattle
Supersonics,
and he isn't even from Seattle.

He is from Cleveland,
by way of Joliet, Illinois.

He always wears that yellow shirt,
the one with the word CAMOUFLAGE
screen-printed on the chest.

His favorite animal is the Seagull.

Need I say more?

Bye, Josh.

If I Had A Nice Nickel

New York goes!
It goes rolling by.
Chicken.
Here ya go, Jingledick,
says Hashem,
thinking Himself hilarious.
Thank you on that.
Sweet inspiration.
Epic nights.
Grow good.
Lightning love-making.
I want to be a good husband.
Finally eating.
Life's poetry and promises.
And breakfast.
As New York goes!
It goes rolling by.
Witnessing me.
In some backseat.
Of a black sedan.
With the window rolled down.
To smiles.

Play It By Ear

Jeroboam, do hamsters have souls?
No idea.
Do they skateboard?
Or tend bar?
Or write?

Many Meditations
   ## in the Hectic Wind

I do my best beat James Dean,
while quoting the emergencies.
Just opened the whiskey and the wine.

The night starts out
like a 90s song.

A good chill in the bones.
Pen and Paper.
Booze.

Even cold wars
have warmer days.

Gallop

Energy, tell me what you need.
I tell you (that) you are a chamber.
tell me everything is better.
in a little fresh kiss forever.

Jump legs and records,
birthday water of whiskey.
smoke in my nose.
there's finally peace down there.

Sing a city song.
commit a crime.
write on the wall in a crooked lie.
And all I want is to wait for your eyes for a
short while

Slain forever in stride.
I used to believe.
I was hollow inside.

Stuck up for years in a story of wine vines.
finally full, she took me away.
with a little bit of good gasoline and
somewhat bad energy.

I wonder no more.
how I can I wonder again.
piano lessons and new guesses and
marvelous mistakes.

I will live.
until I die.
running at full gallop towards the silly-
minute finish line.

What's it like in Washington?
What's it like in reason?

Stop Fires Fast
with Lasagna and Coors Light

Diet city noise,
Making no sense,
in rain town,
Meet your lover in the truck.

after trekking with the best grey clouds,
I live here among the glass
waiting to be baffled,
this is my rough town.

it is not evening raining
but the wind is spooky
as I listen
through window points-of-
views with tigers with one eye each.

Poem

I crack my back
in the hallway
and laugh
about hallways.

Go reach your point
of view
when
we find a way.

I Must've Left the Refrigerator Door Open a Little Bit

God,
I can't wait to shit
times ten!

 This morning is a
great title for a poem,
only
I really did leave the refrigerator open a
bit…

for the whole night.
I was the last one of the couple
left awake last night.

Thankfully,
I was the first of the couple to wake this
morning.

I had to pee.

I went to get a bottle of water,
and I noticed the fridge open,
and the first water
wasn't as cold as it should be.

The storm was still barking. Loud.
Hurricane Sandy.

I looked out the kitchen window
just in time to see a branch come off the big
tree
in the backyard.
The wind was picking up but it was not
raining.
I heard a siren, somewhere.
I made my way back to bed,
stubbing my toe in the hallway.
I never told the other half.
About the refrigerator door, the storm, or the
stubbed toe.
Now I sing folk songs in my head that
always remind me
to close the fucking fridge
all the way,
one stanza.

Dear Danger

Keep me low.
Keep me blue.
Keep me safe
Inside of you.

Poem of Mixing

It starts off
like a late 90s song
and one day
we will be gone.

But for now,
with steal-cupped hands full
of the Pacific Ocean
 we drive across country and throw it in the
Atlantic.

SOAP notes

drinking a beer
and eating a black plum
on the stoop,
noon o'clock.

everyone under
the Wednesday sun
always asks me to
pen a poem for them.

well, here ya go,
you jackyls.
bricks under feet,
forgiveness is exhausting.

I am just
an honorable imposter
of the wayward day,
and the post office is calling my name.

On Science, On Strings

retired from all apathy,
someone sewed my arms back on.
almost as small as days,
and always as big as nights.

the fact that we are always waking up.

and I,
I hope that you are alive.

yawning in some weird honor,
no longer idle in my ideals.
teeth in my shoulder,
distracted in my music.

good at making.

Mispelled Deth

everything moves,
but nothing stays
in motion
forever...

I broke a mug while doing the dishes.
one of a two-piece set
that I got for her;
it [had] a peacock on it.

and it looked more like a giant tea cup
than a traditional flat-bottomed mug.

the other mug is now an only-child.

...I left the water running to pen this poem.

Scissor

we fight like artists,
drunk on porches,
using words
we used
when we were small
at times.

the neighbors
probably hate us,
but fuck them.
no one will write books
about the quiet couple
across the hall.

while god, or God,
is off somewhere singing
his own praises,
we are here on her earth,
trying our best
at living.

Beer List

Despite Gruner for KJ,
we have
Victory Golden Monkey,
Lefthand Sawtooth Ale,
Flying Dog Gonzo Porter,
Ommegang Scythe and Sickle,
and
Breckinridge Christmas Ale.

The Boulevard and the Hum
of Your Heart

we carry plums as gaffers
on a movie set…
this is our movie,
we guess.

we can close the windows if we want to.
doubt and disbelief.
missing the radio.
for all it is worth.

all we can do is live.
and guess at the days.
the ones we aren't guaranteed to see.
trust in this.

I see the streets
the same as you.
Yes, you.
Whomever is reading this shit.

go touch the boulevard
and have a pretty girl
hold your heart
while you sing.

Tell Me That Shit
When I Can Kiss You

the horn and the tomorrow
sound more like
the harp and today,
but the way I live
sounds more like a forgotten
Thursday.

so just give me a heads up
and I will give you my lips,
not to mention the memories
that go along with it.

Celebrate or Riot

I was tending bar
on the last night of the world.

Closed captions,
fuck Kansas and Kentucky!

Well, shit, isn't this funny?
Gleaming unfortunate futures.

Rake the bastards!

There are other men who have won
the Pulitzer,
and I cry mine
almost always
above 23rd street.

Hand me a crush over the phone.
I wish things weren't important
to me.

I missed some speech.

Headaches Have a Way

that's
why goodnight.

I am gonna bleed my
trembling knuckles
while I can't be me
and
I can't change the channel.

Oh, you Poet-King,
She says,
then disappears
into the happy afternoon,
blue in the face
after blowing me.

that's
why goodnight
in the morning
sounds better than goodbye breakfast sheep.

Hell

Hello, inside-of-my-chest,
how are you handling the heat?
Don't leave me to hear alone,
singing about home.

I Drove a Motorcycle Tonight

I do not view any of this lightly.
take a picture of me as I fall down the stairs.
I did not know I am not invincible.
You're so good looking.

my eyes water to tea and confidence,
the houses fly by,
your silent thunder matches mine.

you can have a bite of my life.
everyone I know is misspelled,
except you.

what the hell do we do,
now--
with the only thing we ever knew?

every sentence in my lives.
there's twenty five thousand things
to do
besides survive.

cursed royal wind, wide open,
on the night of the nurse and the criminal,
the exit lane is better

by way of funny architecture.

thank on the starlet sky,
where the old stars die
and the young stars burn.
the rocks and the trees,
the lonesome dreams,
going back in time and going fast
for as long as I can last,
while the docks and the ships without names
let me be me by deeper water,
and a different place.
I've got a plan.

Sometimes

life is fun.
And then sometimes.
it's not fun and then it is fun again.
And then it is not fun.
And then it is fun.
And then you run into your ex-girlfriend.
And then you have to do laundry.
And then it is fun again.
For a second or four.
And then you lose your wallet
At a casual dining restaurant in Chicago.

That is the Straw

juicy memoirs
written by cup-day jerks,
like myself,
about drinking Pepsi,
about being up to no good.

eye diseases ask me to be.
I say
I never wear shoes
without socks,
never use words I can't afford.

you are the only one,
worst for west for snakes from the ground,
while I use sticks I find in the park
to stab at my teeth,
smiles get me drunk.

knives are yardsale fuckers,
with *forever* staining the blade,
and love is lava,
and forever only lasts
until we die for the last time.

I'll Be Her Bruise

I said I had to turn my phone off,
even though I have never turned my phone
off
for a flight for as long as
I have had a cellular telephone.

I took a Xanax and turned to *The Heart is a
Lonely Hunter*.
turbulence be damned by my mouth
and my future son,
for I am not destined to die with these
people.

I cross your beautiful roman features
and I am never eager to shut your eyes,
but keep them open and steady your ears
to our irresistible luxury, our animal.

airplanes land, sometimes,
tell me your thoughts on sleeping liberty,
your gorgeous thighs are marionettes,
yesterday we talked so long about your
favorite song.

the windows are open

and winter is depressed to begin,
because waking up without you
is like drinking from an empty cardboard
box.

I may have been a liar
and I know I have been a fool-hearted fool,
a blue-wallet bastard belonging to your love,
with joy and regret and violas and the
sniffles, but I hum for you perfect.

Fifty Grand for an Idiot

I take off my sunglasses
in the kitchen.
I put a kettle on.
I am unworthy,
so I dance.

no artificial sweetners.
do you know me?
I don't even *know* me.

tea and time,
both drank in the window
while watching the world's leaves
leave like spirit in wind.

where did ya' go?
experiencing new soups.
to find the humming of a new spring.
I am always thinking thoughts of you.
even in kitchens.
while drinking tea.
in yesterland's riverhill clothes.
I will (gladly)
lose my mind
everytime.

Noble Animal

I don't want to do what I am supposed to do.
I shake violently.
With a sick shadow of pure pain in the belly
of my soul.
But I don't cry.

There is snow outside.
I am mixed up in Manhattan.
While he died in a motorcycle accident.
in Orlando fucking Florida.

I don't want to believe it.
The first friend.
To die.

He was the strongest dude I have ever
known.

Cadence

I give you these songs
as you walk away in red jacket...

percussion,
under snow
in Union Square...

so take care of them, those legs
and get unfrustrated,
I wanna marry a figure skater.

Faraday Cage

unexpected *Oopsies* stand tall
against low walls.

make someone else feel dirty instead.

I'm taking back the bench
and the kismet,
and *St. Joseph's*.

I don't want anything
to shake this shape away.
it's a good circle,
so lift me up like a banner candle.

The Fuck Are You Doing Tonight?
(*Co-Written by Eric Schmidt*)

Oh, Arkansas Luke,
we coat the day before the feast,
as if I knew you'd sit across from me
and sigh.

The lady with the lazy hazy apple nostrils
kept telling me dirty jokes
at the kids table.

Therefor your bringing sadness is alone
relief.

Brilliant by dearth and fire,
trouble seems to trombone this old world
and her heckfire lips never change.
Let's go look for a McDonald's.

I have to go pick up my invalid mother.
Her Uncle Rob wears a dress.
Fog makes me sneeze.
Henry fell off the house last year, no one
cared.

For good or ill.

Free From Legacy

the night brings adventure
by circles on the subway,
on a train,
on a bench.

I got hit by a train
while working by the window
of a folk music café
in Union Square.

I was taking a chance,
while the night died.

our laugh is outside for the first time.

Scotch Sour Films

without music,
life would be a mistake.
So Nietzsche says.
I say,
punch yourself
and
live a little.

keep me awake in life's fading light.

I wear a blue wool shirt,
curious as shit,
and a cardigan, of course,
and jeans,
always jeans.

all hale to the drinking man
and the scene;
it's all restaurants,
and bars:
wine and whiskey and beer.

I'll show you some dailies
at dusk.

Songs at Bars Are Kind of Like Time Machines

Delta Spirit comes on at a bar,
and I am transported back to the fall of
2009,
where wrong decisions made me good.

Those days are dead;
those days were murdered by us.

The air is different these days,
tastier in my lungs.

The Bowery Ballroom is still there,
still black, still red with night.
Devendra was just there.
Toots and The Maytals are coming in
December.

I still have a beard,
the second best decisions I've ever made.
The first is moving to New York City.

I still have a beard
at 3:21
on this hearing morning,

surprised at the cost
of memories.

Hello, my old heart,
I draw a sword on a cocktail napkin,
let loose the forgetful tomorrow.

This Side of Amsterdam

me and Fabian,
and a foul-mouthed baby
are gonna be in the front row
for this dancing Saturday.

thanks for the inspiration,
and the sound of the river,
and the atlas,
which I use everyday to find my way.

the face of that place
and the nicks in the glass sky,
night is a windshield,
my hands are waiting for cold dark.

will you be there?
I will be wearing something called
Crazy-About-You.
look for me.

Little Castles Left In A Sketchbook

maybe it is bricks.
maybe it is mortar.
maybe it is now.

you,
the wily past,
kill me tangled,
while red dressed whisper whistles
as if
to
leave me in the destined dark,
the good kin night,
that makes any tomorrow great,
no matter the obstacle course.

Tall Brick Road Hill

I came to country
in lovely love songs
in a beer bar
in Manhattan.
Of all places,
this tall tale place
has thoughts
as red as blood.
Godspeed, to folklore
like this,
brothers being better
and the world
getting warmer.
What a good, sleepy time.
On top of a hill,
somewhere with eyes shut.
Marianne won't go to sleep tonight
until really late.
The metronome clicks.
This city is more Americana.
I go to pieces.
Come and take the sleep out of my night.

Boo Hop

I'd still be living
if it weren't for you.

Get dirty.
Get clean.
Get bled.

Worth everything,
the day has.

The hardest things are black and white.
I write poems about love.
It's a think like dancing in habit.

Octopus Wrists

that was a helm child,
falling over forever.

I am glad I am not the leader tonight.

the girl with the wrists.
cold and sick.

Patch Me Over to the General

today was weird,
too much thread,
two hours dead,
but the Chinese food was good.

I was something,
something of piss and vinegar,
of guesses.
Fuck Brooklyn forever.

I hate not wearing sunglasses
on the rumbler.
I somehow always forget
the danger of a beautiful stranger.

A Poet Gross in Atlantic City

sneezing hard,
tasting blood
on the very ugly casino carpet,
installed inexpertly
for kid-sickos and black jack bimbos.

and me.

look for the thought of the world
before curtains and webs and energy,
where sleepless nights live long.
back to the school
of beautiful losers,
weighing heavy on Formica hearts,
uninstalled unknowingly
for the killers with the coloring books.

and me.

see the swinging lights,
tangled up and tongue-tied,
writing this red life.
the boardwalk is there,
but I never laid eyes on it.
wasting nights is syntax art.

Durable; A Heavy

Adjectives are above
eating high schools,
I always want to see.

This Thanksgiving was not in Rhode Island.
Our Thanksgivings have never been in
Rhode Island.
But July has the Folk Festival
just for us.

River of Noise

I'll take my licks
early
as a brute witness,
a criminal song,
a waitress.

Better than in the summer,
there are paper clips scattered
along 88th street.

Each one belongs to the morning.
I don't belong to the morning.

Maybe I will
tomorrow.

Metal Forks

pillow cases are something.
figure out a cure for me.
it's been four years since I broke my head.
it's been four years and it does not end.

no talker,
I want to dance until you hold me.
you know my songs.
I want to hear your keys in the door.

won't see a light;
plastic forks in a plastic bag.
leave a girl whose name is not Marie.
I plan to be forgotten when I am gone.

I Am Dedicated

I would sell my shoes to the moon just to
keep you dreaming.

I just walked into a vision of jazz life,
along the border of your guns
and I am just a blind man
that drinks the rain
and waits for lightning strikes
to design strangers
for me to fall in love with…

A Tiny Little Uzi

do you ever look at your own hands
and think
that the world is going to end?

hold the gun tight
like a guitar
or an unarmed infant.

hope you slept well
where troubles be gone
and ghosts don't bounce checks.

no rocks or salt or nails,
there is a sign up the hill
and it says This Way Next.

The Next Time Around

The 4 train.
Sunglasses and folk music.
Something sick.
Maybe hungover.
Not Spanish.
Fatties eat pizza and black-and-white
cookies
on this Rumbler,
makes me hungry then sick.
Their eyes are pretty,
but they are ugly.
I remember this train
from another life.
I used to take it to the N train
and then to Herald Square.
I met a girl there.
I miss these adventures,
in which all parts were roses
and distant dreams
that she used to mop the floor.
The next time around
I will do the dishes differently.
Never have I felt such numbing, torching
truth.
I exit at Union Square.

I sit on a bench.
Say goodbye to the blue afternoon.
Say hi to the crackheads and the squirrels.
Sit for a second.
Sit for forever.
I never knew I was a lover.

Titan-Like

I am not from Michigan.
Reinvent my name.
I wear old boots.
I goof in the polluted wind.

Name me as your lover.
I thought I could be anything.
Mornings are doublewide.
I am the king.

Guitar my silly, stupid heart.
While I walk upon the river.
I design lightning.
Throw it at curtains.

You dance on these pages.
Like lovely spider webs.
My savior and my sin.
Run, just run.

Grey or Green

I have one-hundred and sixty two tigers
and they are tied to gold strings.
Your eyes blame me for the sun going down.
Your eyes blame me for everything.

I stink.
Yes, I do.
The tigers like my living rooms.
I have a thousand ways to try.
My red eyes are grey
and her green eyes are looking beyond my
palace shoulders
at a boy trying better that I.

Trying to catch the train.
Trying to dodge the snowflakes.
The snowflakes are in the shape of his face.
His face is now mine.
My eyes change colors.
Yellow is the color of my despair.

Cinnamon Toast Crunch.
Breakfast is the most important.
I walk in the city forever.
There is no real goodbye.

Canis Latrans

that lamb
bleeds good blood.
don't be innocent.
be a warpath.

Hey, Old Cold Hands!

half the rent
times half the bar
times girls
minus life.

death is common
and
love is a lost cause.

vowels change
and
I am still
amazed
that I am still
alive.

I knock my teeth
for eternity
and breakneck speed.

Ladd's Addition

across the river
where the white people live
when songs turn into lonely bones
shattered on the floor.

my body is weak,
I am worried it might just leave.
Portland, be my symphony asleep,
be my last summer.

The row houses.
The mornings never fail on desire.
Still innocent.
Still speak of nights living.

I pour wine
for trickster women
and their wandering eyes;
I am invested out here.

(put my pants on backwards)

stunned
by animal legs
and animal eyes.

shocked
by jumper cable lips
and razor sharp hips.

caught
by wrists and collar bones
and December stars.

built by a butcher,
I guess I am easily forgotten.

the short answer is
yes.
the long answer is
when.

saved
by a solid symphony
and winter, always.

The Hollow Hot Month of May

I live until I believe.

Running, Wild

I go to the bank.
I spit on the subway tracks.
I am hungry.
I am in love.

I step on the train.
Like an East Coast Emperor in flannel.
I split curtains.
I eat good.

I clobber people.
With weird, selfish poetry.
Like this.
Everyone hold on tight.

My body breaks.
With the beginning of every song.
Check your wrist.
If you've had enough of this.

The sun will rise.
And the moon will shine.
And I will call today mine.
It ends without a shout.

Hindsight is colorblind.
This is the halfway mark.
Do you know what I mean?
Trying to fight the in-between.

Warm Beers

best enjoyed
by morning,
it's safe to say
we have all had
family issues.

whistled this way in the spring
in our killer cousins' backyard
with an archaic set of swings.

video cassettes are buried there,
along with nameless hamsters,
and glass for your sister's wrist.

catch the fossils
of a garden
with electric uncle boots.

the ending is overplayed
and soon begins another day.

The Leaves Remind Me of a Shortcut

Let's stay awake and listen to the sky.

Don't just hear this song,
listen to its world and wind.

from the end of silence,
see the sun come rising,
and life begins to fly.

I don't want to close my eyes.

The Stage

she's on Wakefield Street
in white pants.
bad choice,
because it is raining.
well, not really.
it's a shitty medium mist
on a cold Sunday in December.

in the distance,
she can see the city
covered in fog
from the neck up.

many years afraid,
she looks like the insane future
of graham-cracker luck,
with a splash of fine gone love.

her head is phones,
her eyes are in dark glasses,
despite the lack of sun, altogether,
because of the gloom
and the Rumbler.

Shadows of Train

lightning by design,
with a soul only so brave.

to an ice skating rink,
the heart must seem like a monster.

I want to call you
from a payphone on 26th Street.

just to be the first
person to ever call you from a payphone.

Kickflip the Sun

in the middle of a song.
walking up the hill.
eating peanuts from a brown paper bag in
my pocket.
and just throwing the shells on the ground.
hearing every mouth on every face talking
about explosions in Boston.

what do you do when everybody on the
street
    is singing like it's Sunday?

it's Monday.
and all I can do is kickflip the sun.
and eat nachos and read poetry.

we are the time.
but no one seems to give a damn.
until something…

Gun Dinner w/ Stupid People

I have tentacles.
They have chairs.

The floor has bullets.

Has the whole world gone mad?
I have no memory of that.

St. Falls, Larger

build a small fire,
and sit close to it.
vinyl is still in,
and Brooklyn is still dangerous.

read this book
for what it's worth.
fifteen bucks,
give or take a nickel or nine.

I know the land
of wooden waters.
your luminous lips
murder me in a free storm.

Movie Trivia

Ghostbusters,
I am your man
with a plan.

GoodFellas,
I sleep between your teeth.
My jeans floss your dreams.

Groundhog Day,
I didn't know what it means to believe.

Good Will Hunting,
I am much bigger than my own little
dreams and preoccupations.

Call me moments not minutes.
We are aircraft.

Mix CD, Blah Blah Blah 6

1. *You and Me* by **Penny and The Quarters**
2. *Switzerland* by **The Last Bison**
3. *I Won't Found* by **The Tallest Man on Earth**
4. The Book of Right-On by **Joanna Newsom**
5. *Confessions of a Futon Revolution* by **The Weakerthans**

Hands of Steel, Heart of Gold

I don't want to write right now.

Flowers bruise, too.

Any Time Soon

are you performing
any
where
in NYC
any
time
soon?

or on earth?

so I can send my friends
to be eyes for me.
some times our friends are good at being our
eyes.

Paper Plate Presentation

ham and cheese
and a PBR
and foggy taxicab windows
at 4:35 am.

this is what it's like.

tomorrow will be dreary
with chance of snow
but tonight is riding
the dusty wings of yardsale love.

get big.
the city is yawning,
and the daily newspapers
are being presented to eyes,
while my eyes need to shut.

the past is checkered.
the holy cab driver and I smile.
he too must've had a fine gone evening.
and no matter what tomorrow loans,
tonight was sexy and swell.

the same time.

Macabre Play

two more days of this and then I will retire.

a gift is given then given up
by...shhh!
let the drum speak to new year's eve.

which is just another night.

hurt both my hands in a gunfight.
the trigger was a knife.

Up a Storm

up a storm,
the invented warm.
no other Autumn
could destroy me like this.
glad you are alive.
you should dance.
and I am not nice.

Tender New Signs

Love is a super future gun.

In a sense, it is real.

Ideas are real.

Not so sure about stars,
Especially the ones on shoulders.

Figments.
Up.

I come from the stupid silly sun.

I am not real.
See through.

I Love Your Teeth

This poem is about eyes.
And hammers.
Both pound
Entropy, respectively.

Breakfast is good.
Book is great.

Make the night go fast.
When I am at work.
Make the night last long.
When I am with her.

The Bar

Only rich people have American Express
cards.
Beer is free in my world.
This is a skateboarding poem.

This Wild Morning

my feet stink.
not as bad as last
summer-time stink.
however,
the sink is clean.
the bathtub, too.

one drink with Garfield
then hitch-hiked uptown.
twist of grace.

dance.
move.
with the speed of light.

goodnight, coloring books.

I keep burning lime juice
in my wrist.

Goodbye to myself
And all the money I could dream.

Rum-and-Coke

She asked me,
"what are you writing about?"
"I'm writing about you," I said.

And the song 'Home'
by Edward Sharpe and the Magnificent
Zeros
comes on at a bar
at the right time
for the millionth time.

That sad sack of shit song came on
and I danced,
like I owned certain
songs and mountains
and moments.

Then I went to the bitch bar
and ordered a rum-and-coke.
And forgot about the dismal night.
I sputtered stand-stills.

And then 'Bushwick Blues' by Delta Spirit
comes on
and destroys my night.

That song makes me possessive.
Rooftops and years
and parks.
I hate lying and being in bars.

There is a certainty.
And one more,
I live concerned
in a bus.
Despite it all, can we fix this life?

Minus the G

Explanation.

how an amount of fear by making laws
for things as these
could somehow subdue
as well as promoting fear...

animals need animals.

Ate By Snakes

I try to save you.
But you don't want to be saved by me.

rip the paper.
save it for later.

Goose, Them & The Irrational

Had I known,
I would have done
a few things differently.

I'm certain every human
in the history of
the fine gone world
who has lost a young friend
turned and burned a bridge.

I'm singing songs about the future.
Wondering where you are.

If Gilbert Were Around

He would drive us to Queens,
take us to The Creek and The Cave,
hit on the bartender,
hit on Wolf
and disappear in an Irish exit.

Socks, a Castle, Some Soup, and a Better Acorn

whisper in ears
the word,
Shout!

my stupid silly arm muscles miss you
like lying lagoons
and gold dabloons
and an afternoon movie on cable,
one that won't let you switch the channel.

unlove the hiccups
on opposite murdered Thursdays,
seventy percent of afternoon sheepish youth.

and I am a gunsmith,
remembering far-away light.

I Have Never Won a Coin Toss

It's snowing.
It's really coming down.
It is yesterday.
In my hard heart.

Wind is free for my bones.
And I lose my wish to drown.
I walk alone and write/carve on a bench.
For fear of silence.

Whenever it snows sideways like this.
I listen to The Tallest Man on Earth.
And walk around Union Square.
Winter was ours.

Obligated Pride

Riding the light
between helping
and hiding.

Wise up and be lonesome.

Listen to Confusion

too tired to write, too drunk to fuck,
I remember the never-ending summer rain.
we're gonna die of lonesomeness
for sure some damn day.

Parachute Kings

we fall to the earth
like songs with seats
and handkerchiefs
on better days
holding autographs
as our only souvenirs.

escape while winter
comes and forgets me,
inside their daring,
catch me if you can.

clouds pass us by
like tourists,
stars are just nicks
in the glass night sky.

We can't go back.

to shirts and years
riding shotgun to lessons
and listening.

This old dark machine
has been here before

made my own town
to explore,
orchards and all.

Protect us from the madness of the future yet
to come.

I wear a hat
and land in the market
with smells and planets.
we start making sense.

growing codes
and inside jokes
in gardens
alongside cherry tomatoes
with the option
to destroy it all.

this is my backyard.
what's more, is that this is
my world on sad brown and blue earth
for days like rain
drops
dropping from the sky
like happy tears.

Let's Go Be Great

I don't know how to write like that.
I called you back.
While I was wearing a Yankees hat.

When your mouth is laying oak.
I will give you flowers and soap.
Begging for the bottom.

Under tongues.
Love comes and all.
Sexy as the word, Lips.

Forgotten like last year's eclipse.
Monster mice chew up your bed.
God is in your head.

Love is in your honey pot heart.
Slick and thick.
I am here, combing your hair.

Feel me in the backs of your knees.
Come inside.
Be fine.

Old Darby Road, Montana

no games now.
Frankly.
just hardware stores.
sorry for the rapids.
and for being an idiot.

the house throws up trees.
the river eats my clothes.
no one I have ever met has even seen a
brand new car.

this year was wet with letdowns.
but dry as far as crops.

horse shit.
stolen guns.
sheep skulls.
I have invented my own math.

windchimes make me happy.
I didn't come here for the fishing.
the mountains scratch the sky.
and make the sun bleed.
Dusk.

I have had a few heart attacks in my time.
fell in love in Dakota.
she shot me down with her revolver.

Drinking a Beer While Taking a Shit

proud like love.
It's raining in this Sunday world,
west of November.
Thank Hashem, this foul year is almost over.
Hope is a currency
and I plan to save
some in a blood bank next summer.
Tidings forget me.
Magazines kill me.
I take off my shirt for this.
My arm muscles miss you.
You said the words but you didn't even
speak.
I gave a lot mostly.
Red art money and revolution blues
look at me sweetly.
New years eve is just another day.
The pressure to be great is great.
Thoughts.
Youngsters make me cry colors.
I lost my mind long ago.
I left on a sweaty Sunday like this
while running late
for work.

Night Library

I am a senator man,
because I miss you.
Candy flipping,
where is Country Luke?
I can't talk
and I cut my heart.

Bad Fried Friend

This world will last forever.
This world will always let you down.

Hopes shouldn't go up.

I can't cancel last night
or my sister's cancer,
but…

The city got quiet real fast.
Palace grin.

I Still Remember That Winter

2010 wasn't.
2011 killed.
2012 flew.

The Rumbler is still the same.

Your room smelled clean
and
recently shaken
like the furniture
had recently been transported.

I miss your starry shoulders.
I cut my finger off.

Window Shopping

Freedom sometimes
is clean and free.
Glaser's Bakery, the smells.
Tending bar next-door.
That invisible organ player
at the Church of the Holy Trinity.
It's notes dance their way outside
and into my waxy ears.
I wave to Wendy the clerk.
I toss terrible jokes at the brown bagel boys.
There are hip teenagers drinking
wine on the corner of White Harlem.
They offer me a slug,
and to their surprise,
I grab the bottle and take my turn.
Thanks, snakes.
New York belongs to me,
and I belong to New York.

Work, Friends, Poetry, and the Blues

we spend the night
like loose dollars lost.
Happy and running
for the maybe train.
Maybe different.
Maybe waiting.
Maybe Brooklyn.
Maybe not.
Work comes with years.
We laugh up lies
with an apologetic tongue.
Kill concern.

Inbuilt

This is 59th street!

Headphones are broken.

Love me as close as you can.
It is hard to remember the end of December.

This is Grand Central!

Hunting cap for all its worth
while hunting human hearts.
Deaf fire,
lakes are lakes, not glowing flowing rivers.

This is Union Square!

Where
benches represent
 the trenches of love.

I Want a Taco

don't you?

I am a tycoon at quitting,
like jewelry getting ripped off by ghosts.

I hope you get eaten by snakes.

When I look in the mirror
I see a stay-at-home sad.

I walked under a ladder
when I needed one.

Poem

Baked a cake in a view
in the forest north.
Not near here.
You'll find us in a VCR.

We run along the river.

It's alright,
the camera speaks
without paintings,
but with cistern proof.

Make me miss you more.

If I Had a Pistol

There are books
we sat aside.

Trains can try,
and I got freaky wavy.

The werd outside
is misspelled and cold.

Reality mixing with the gaudy middle,
I sat my pulse to East Coast time.

I am small-town,
but not enough.

A Poetry Reading on a Rooftop on the Eve to New Year's Eve

with hands reversed,
I hit a shirt and picked the words out
of a bale of hay.

leave like leaving is me.
brunch was a possibility,
but it ended just in time.
ice on the stoop steps
and I almost ate shit.

took a cab
which took the goddamn FDR.

all the way there.

when I got there,
all the cool criminals were there,
shivering and pretending
in the Brooklyn wind.

I could see the steeples of the city
over ugly brown Bushwick crests.
I wanted just to die.
or somewhere else to hide.

bad red wine and of course PBRs
and bad breath Bobs,
reading bad poems about bad sex,
and a bad ska band
cut short by spit valves.

I straighten out my shoulders
and simply looked up at fallen stars,
while reading my own bad poems
about chocolate chip cookies
and rivers
and sharp hips
and sweet dreams.

I felt useless up there.

I finish.
The applause lets me down.
I look over the roof's edge
and apologize to the ground,
six stories down.

I'm wearing two pairs of socks
and I wish you were here.
Listen to confusion.
Shy Shy misses the set,
shows up late with Renee.

My legs are freezing.
No whiskey.

You are my favourite colour.
The yellow harp on the edge
of the told world,
untold to be me and my saints,
and two days from now
the fine gone world will be different.

These

I sigh in a field of tired horses
with silly things
forevermore.

There's a fawn in all my
dreams without numbers.

Uncle Ice Cream Truck Presents

I was waiting there,
swimming through apologies.

I still live
and walk
with legs
and thoughts.

There is a hawk
somewhere
doing the same, wow.

Fire, Fire, Knives!

Bury your knives in fire
and forget about me forever.

I make a movie
from within:
everything I have ever wanted.

I wrote about narrowness
and birds
and you.

I give life a name.

Punch me in tongues.

Pretty Brunette on The Rumbler

The next stop is Union Square.
I've been there.

She sees me and I see her
and we both wish
things were different.

Just a Little Dance for You

Visceral Sam dances
with no man
but Miles Davis.

Her body is like
broken liquid.

I watch via YouTube,
from Florida,
and I am forever changed,
inspired by time and art,
and art and time.

The Hawks That Pencils Make

save our eyes for snacks.
this is yesterday's yesterday hair.
so get oval.
and.
shock a home.
metaphors are talons.
so I wrote.

we topped the shadows of a silver hill.
ourselves historic.
made markings in the field.

we made time.
while the air was light.
studying the horizon with our ticklish feet.
living like pilots.
we sleep in lines.
like these.
just drawings of hope and how we forget.

trees w/ scars.
in the shape of young hearts.
initials and arrows.

get over it all.

and this then.
write a Greek curse.
hold on to every word.
we don't want to know.
where we are meant to go.
this is a green-eye adventure.

we wished in silence.
but sang in yonder youth under skies
while the grass still turned with the Earth
where the birds are right to fly.

I'd Drive You Home If I Could Find My Car Keys, But I Don't Have a Car

I only had one beer.
and I've been bored
since my buddies dragged me here.

Decent dive in Louisville,
but Mondays are mine.
And then you walked in,
I said I liked your knit cap,
and you said thanks,
and then I asked if I could buy it off you.

You laughed,
and I said I was serious.

You said "Buy me a beer and we'll
negotiate."
Brilliant.

Brunette.
Small.

Called Charlie,
sick short for Charlotte.

Laughter is love.

And I never saw you again.

Pine Trees Deserve More Than Me

The cadence of me
combined with the wind
makes wonderful wishes
and
these wishes are asking
for 'more wishes'
but
 the brighter we burn, the younger we get
and then things end.

Pine trees
See.

Why don't we fall in love?

Explore

some more.

let the crow call your morning.
I like mountains.
fuck the Atlantic Ocean.
I am younger than the sun.

decide what our necks are doing.
and finally.

what happens in caves?
all sorts of stuff happens in caves.

witness how that light makes you beautiful
again.

nothing we've seen has been mapped.
the moons and the marigolds.
dogs are walking across the room.
somewhere.
on two legs.
west and east.

still sweating out secrets.
still looking throw the trees.

searching.
for something.
we are there and then we are not.

Time Falls

Still friends with Abby Lavey
She seems to be doing well in Wyoming.
It's crazy how life happens.
I saw Can't Hardly Wait with her
In a theater on University and Goldenrod.
My sister dropped me off.
He dad owned a restaurant
In that shopping center
If I remember correctly
But there is good chance
That I don't remember correctly.
I do remember kissing her
And I know I am glad we are still friends
No matter how distant.

Same Page, Same Stance

Writing some shit.
Wish it was as good as yours.
Wish I were a better skateboarder.
Proud? Me? Sure.

You're the only one.
For me.
I know.
Love is a drug and a fakie heel flip.

But I gotta get you back some how.
And I might still be falling.
In Washington Square Park.
But that's okay.

These Tribute Nights

Just got off the train,
eating a goddamn Gluten-free
oatmeal blueberry muffin
and feeling manly.

Bleecker and Bowery,
Lawrence Ferlinghetti tribute at the Yippie,
and I'm getting ready to leave NYC,
maybe for good, or ill.

These walls, these people,
like a weird old asylum;
this is my number.

Curved ceiling,
stages, odd adorable,
up and down,
capitol Poets and odd smells.

Too luminous,
these people are ghosts,
real ghosts.

This is where people read
bags of skin

through beards;
no booze.

Some guy is paying for a latte with nickels.
There is a table in my kitchen
without legs,
but I sit at it.

These people are dead again.
Abby Hoffman would be furious.
I hear cats.

Seriously, cats, coming from the basement.
They are furious too.
And sad.
And singing.

Franco showed up,
but I don't remember inviting him.

Oh well,
welcome to my world,
Garfield Twists.

Why'd that guy call me Richard?
Some old dude called me Richard and shook
his finger at Franco.

Why do old dudes always have bad breath?

Born gone,
she came, arrived,
just to see me read,
and then she left.

And I watched her walk past the big front
window
in a red canvas coat.

Vanished.
Beautiful.

Out of Her

eat a Koala Bear
and shut the fuck up.

eat a sandwich,
and watch spring bases,
while eagles happen
and assholes live.

she hates me
back on the rooftop,
and it's ok,
kickass hawks the horizon,
while the rest of us breathe bad dreams.

cracked black pepper,
and sisters,
and sadness,
forgive us for finger,
and I trust you,
but my trust doesn't trust me.

Poem

Succumb
to days, minutes, moments,
maggots, foes, forever,
and ever.

Hope is a price,
untradeable.

45 mins.
Let's go to the CD shoppe.

I want to go swimmin' with ya'.
I want to go swimmin' with ya' at night.

This ain't no sad folk song.

Gentlemen, please,
think back a year and just see what ya' hear.

Thick in Brooklyn

I have been good at falling down stairs
for many years, no poltergeist can stop me,
even with the help of the concrete floor
that cradled my head.

my bedroom has pits and peril,
animals and haunts
that taunt me and the way
I love.

that's why I always say
something like this poem
and that weapon,
both bloody, good fun.

Poem About The Last Poem

I brush my teeth twice in a row.
I do some blow.
I leave for the poetry gig.
Stopping at the grocery pig.

The subway platform is hot as hell.
My eyes melt.
Inside the train, Jesus Freaks.
They're freaking me out.
I switch cars.

I listen to Jollie Holland songs.
Through earbuddies.
I transfer at 59th to the N train.
I stick my tongue out at a little.
Black baby who can't help but stare.
At the weird-looking poet with the beard.

That kid gets it.
The world, simple.
He laughs when I stick out my tongue.
Finally, I get off the train at W. 4th.
I walk up police stairs.
And past forgotten Queens from Queens.
Left on Cornelia Street.

I am there.
In that basement.
I half listen and take a shot of whiskey.
Peter tells me bad breath secrets.
Tom isn't there.
Bob Hart is.
Hala is there.
I dig her stuff.
And her legs.

My name is called.
I read a poem called
"Rambutan Minnow Reprise".
I get off stage
and take another shot of whiskey.
And then disappear.
Without paying my tab.
I walk right.
I go into Grey Dog Café and feel uncool.
Matt English is there.
He gives me a beer and cheers me up.
We snort Ketamine in the bathroom.
I feel nothing.
I leave and walk East on Bleecker.

This is good enough for my great grandpa.
I have to bartend tomorrow.

The train home is delayed.
I am late.
My lady is pissed.
I don't care.

I'm glad I am here.

mind kill the robot factory

I'm heading out west,
got some tending to do
there.

wrap my wrists
in bracelets and time,
otherwise I don't know how I'd find my way
back.

my strong hands
are still
needed there,
clapping.

for the long run,
and wrung necks,
mistakes indeed make us rich

I'll bring the winter back with me,
mama don't you cry,
tomorrow ain't gonna die despite how hard I
tried.

Bright Silence

She picked me up from the Kansas City
International Airport
in a Kia.

Silence from our mouths,
and I recognized the music immediately.
A band called Blind Pilot
was singing about peacocks.
We remained silent
and just held hands
under steering wheels.

The highway was a magnificent work of art.
The lights played symphonies on the asphalt
and the horizon saw as far as Utah.
No buildings in the way.
A few casual dining restaurants.
She took my hat off and threw it in the
backseat.

I forgot about my hat and never got it back.
I hope it is still bright and silent
somewhere in Kansas.

...And Always Will Be

Put your eyelashes on
and feel beautiful
even though you already are.

Making movie quotes
in a city that will never
let me go.

Under the lights
at the river
or lack thereof.

We will seek up and out,
two fountains found,
waiting to be uncivilized water, regardless.

I hope your heart
is good
and strong.

Because
I love your hands,
and they are pretty clean.

This is a Bunch of Bullshit I Wrote While At A Rock-N-Roll Show One Night

Petrified wood heart!
Devil bastards!
Country Luke is late.
Vernon is late.
Matt English is late.
I am on time.
She is early.

Where we were going,
I had no idea.
Past tense.

My love is undoubtedly wasted on
tomorrow's tonight,
on hiking and looking at rivers;
ghosts watch me be a frogman for some
frogwoman,
for some reason.

I can be your ferriswheel
or your restaurant,
or your Ferris Bueller,
and you can be my doctor.

I feel like I am always getting weaker.

the sun is shining brighter
sometimes
but the quesadillas are microwave warm.

joy, soul.

That is all.

Recognize This Poem

this.
is.
the.
way.
that.
I.
believe.
in.

this.
Is.
The.
Way.
That.
I write.

I got no pay poem,
but I eat your soul.
I peeled it off the street
on which I skate
with my tongue
like a sheet or magic carpet.

I have a blacksong heart,
and I can't control my national self.

Sundays, I tend the bar.
I have been running for so long,
but I didn't get very far.

my white knuckles are bleeding
from punching valet parkers in the head
in Montreal and in Chicago and in Montreal
again
and LA and Miami.

A path of bourbons, Manhattans, and
scotches...

the air conditioner in front
stops, craps-out, just as 4am starts,
and I am too drunk to tinker with it,
besides I am writing
Buddhist bullshit about existentialism,
so I pull a sideline of white from the
emergency kit
and do a little bump.

I was beside myself with delight.

when will it be winter?
in winter time.
when will it be less?
in longer lines.

I don't know
if the knife-nicks in the sky
are aligned tonight
or will be when we're middle-aged.

I know time.
once in a while.
I know hearts beat too fast.

further north
than south,
aforementioned
in emails.

Poemless.

if I died
right fucking now,
coyote blood would
chop your fucking heart
in half,
and my love
will hold you tight,
and the kids
are never going to be right,
and they will never find us.

the end of your aching life,
will be water-logged.

Mark Hill, please
kill my werdz.

Lastnight's two-night.
I was right.

photographs of stories
and the years inside of them
and certain days,
not the bad days,
trapped in pretty bows,
and the smell of the backs of knees
and the north star, I guess.

my eyes feel weird.

I cut my socks in half,
half way through the day,
too hit-hot, insulated ankles,
hung out with a Gerard man.

Free from bloodcells and cellular phones.

I would cry if I could fly.

honey shepherd!
and god is dead,
goodnight,
he said.

in the nighttime
when you feel me
in the backs of your knees,
I will be here.

in cocaine nightmares
on rooftops in midtown Manhattan,
I sink into trying birthdays
and dark texts, goodbye.

I don't know any body
who wants to be here.

I'll let you know.

If I do.

our hearts are breaking themselves in.
this tired night
and every tired night.

I slam cabinet doors,
everywhere,

out of spite.

tornados
are losers.

Indie music and blue Monday skinny jeans
for Tuesday advantages,
and anti,
alas(!),
I have found my thumbs.

pont,
the bridge is not silent.
I am the name.
of several places.

Back in time.
Some Januarys snap.

this should be the beginning of a poem:
I wish I were 21!
with a gun.

my friend, Christopher Nicholas Corso,
was there.

That was ten years ago

In some dreams
God died in his sleep

with…

blue bandages.
Easter vomit.
Bad blow.
better.
bathtub full of puppies,
all called Bob Dylan.

This is
A far cry
from a restart.

it is 6pm on the west coast.
bloody boogers.
another tomorrow looming.
laughs in branches.
find yourself, fast.
stealing with gloves made of red yarn.

What happens to ourselves
upon yonder death, the end.

No one asks me this.

I don't know.
Probably nothing.

god died in his sleep.

"I'm at my folks house, goodnight."

Goon

I am just a fine gone goon
that grew up skateboarding
and listening to punk rock music
and ska.

I don't differentiate
between love and hate,
emotions are appetites.

I eat.
You eat.

Rambutan Minnow Reprise

while
I am New York,
I am slower
than its pulse.

this is a city of quickness
and consequence;
there is a lot happening,
but nothing going wrong in the night
of mine.

everything that happens is suppose to
happen.

aforementioned evenings
are not empty,
by damages are the stars
in the sky,
this is what's happening:

while
plot twists happen
everyday, cleverly,
by Hashem's finger...

and all we do is wait to die.

while
epic,
under nicks
with loose fangs
and windows,
we try sitting still,
happily being nothing's anatomy.

while
at the center of the universe,
we dance in rain
and say the werd Motherfucker
too much to receive approval
from a creature holding an empty stone gun.

while
swimming under trees,
and wishing for restarts
our hearts sometimes melt
away.

while
folks and goondykes
live Fridays on Prairies
in the middle of America,
we are here.

her parents say this place is beautiful;
her brother is in a basement in midtown
doing blow and going.

while
good nights sleep,
the city weeps.

while
the moon mentions you,
I do, too, in printed words
just these motherfucking symbols.

while
inchworms inch along
to a whiskey song,
we will be here,
unliving.

this place is haunted
and this chair is falling apart.

I am the writer
and these are the people.

after her shift at the hospital,
she ate Xanax and toast for dinner.

she needs this poem
oh-so-bad.

foster the lifer in nutty pukeness,
and nuking potatoes,
only to bite them
then throw them.

Tired

Jones cut a line in the snow
with his French boots.

This side was his,
the other side was summertime.

Tiny Terry takes walks alone in Carl,
the sir cure park,
glades on high, above black river,
and Tiny is a renegade
of some sad kind,
that sometimes
goes to dinner alone
and movies alone.

But the weird thing
is she honestly ain't sad.

He is a new uncle.
Tuesday night,
she wrecked a rental car.

Names don't matter anymore.

There is a party on the G train.

myself,
two bottles of wine,
music and torchlight,
and I am Paul Revere.

Tornado Fire Face

Is she the winner
that walks down the streets,
four pearls to five toes,
and dancing vegetarian...

To my chest, can she be the best...

Probably not...

But probably amazing.

Spin Cycle

did laundry this morning.
salted the stoop.

I'm scared of slipping and falling.
Choking alone.

eat that metaphor.
as leftovers.

the sun was whispering.

about.

reasons that.
fly at your face.
like copper from a penny gun.

and.

tornados find us.
when we are kicking stones.
searching for treasures.
on the sidewalks.
with our heads down.
and our eyes on the ground.

try.

to keep your attention.
on dimes in the sky.
not nickles.
heads up.
upon won earth.

where we simply spin.

unless.

we turn around.
and talk.
to the past.
telling it to leave.
us.
alone.

life is funny when you search.

Take Care and See Ya Soon

We are going west for the weather.
We have a thousand delights.
Just give us time.
My plans are in you.
My hands are in your hands.
Be my gold mine.

This is a sentence of repentance.
Forgive last night like forever.
Write like the pages will burn.

Let's listen to rap songs.
And forget about rights and wrongs.

West coast in weak week.
Let's steal the smile from the sun.
Forget about fun.
And just live.

Poem

I want to be free.
I want to be low.
But I want to go higher.
I have never taken a nap in my life.
I don't think I will make it through another
year let alone another night.

There's a Bird in the Bar

130 taps of craft beer.
Big open windows welcome the summer.
The summer forgets me always.

There is a commotion in the corner.
My right; your left.
The devil's up.
God's down.

A little bird found his or her way
into the bar.

People are panicking, women are running.
It's just a fucking bird.
It's more nervous than you fucking hipsters.

I excuse myself and take a shot of whiskey.
I catch it by simply putting out my
benevolent hand and letting it land.

I take it outside of everyone's lives.
I say goodbye and watch it fly.
In circles. Forever friends.

Seattle has me tense.

Pissing in the Wind

Afternoon, pissing in the wind.
Funny mosquitoes and big beers.
Periods.
Writing poems about tips.
Lost my shirt to Ben Affleck.
It's definitely summer or somewhere.
I took the bus downtown.
To the record store.
There was an Asian gal on the bus.
Carrying a puppy.
A yorkie.
I hate her.

The record store was closed.
Ran some errands.
Went to the camera store.
The camera store was closed.
Rain.
Bob's antiques.
Escape.
Forced lunch.
Not a hundred percent today.
Anxiety is a mystery.
Some days ya' just wake up at half.
Mentally and mentally.

I decided to walk back.
Across Burnside bridge.
Hoping the fresh air would do me good.
But the heat suffocated me.
My sister would tell me to take off my
flannel.
But I would decline, respectively.
Reggae show tonight.

Mix CD, 1016, Montreal, Quebec

1. *Final Days* by **V for Escargot**
2. *Of Love* by **Dyan**
3. *Written Over* by **Miles Benjamin Anthony Robinson**
4. *True Love Will Find You in the End* by **Daniel Johnston**
5. *Wapusk* by **Kathleen Edwards**

Boycott the Bullshit

riding on the back of a Vespa,
hanging on tight to a girl called Somewhere
whose blonde hair is whipping me
in the face, along with the raw rain;
it smells like shampoo and petrichor.

we are heading to a party
with some of her high school friends.
doesn't matter, but they have a mini ramp
in their backyard so my skateboard
is strapped to my backpack.

in spite of kickflips, I wonder
how she will introduce me to her tribe,
and I wonder what dudes will be jealous of
me,
because confidence is a killer
especially bohemian lately, and hatred is
sexy.

once there, I plan to dance and kiss her neck
twenty thousand times, avoiding PBRs
in place of rock and roll on the ramp
where I will air the grill and make everyone
laugh,

because I am only good at two or three
things.

we will leave early, because...
well, because of love, skateboarding,
and making strangers laugh,
while the stars stay still
and we're not supposed to be.

Awayfromhomework:
Rain and Woods

There's no rain
in these woods
that we call the world.

strawberries in the Portland there-you-go.
I trade time for looks, in exchange for
bastard books of poetry.
I give you the world and the word of the
burning seagull,
from where it came,
I have no fucking idea.
portland.
with gutter punks
on every corner.

It's a long way from the seder.

Growing Up in Orlando

Not everything was Disney, trust me.
Don't make me laugh.
Shit gets ghetto there.
Just ask Chris Corso or Dan Groen.

For a while there.
All I had was skateboarding.
And a little drugs.
Before the GoodFellas saved me.

You can confirm this.
With Mark Hill.
Maybe Joe Clatworthy.
If he isn't being stupid.

I am happy to have that place.
That town.
That is much more than Mickey.
But I was more than happy to skate to NYC.

I'll Tell Ya' When Ya' Dial Me Up

publishing books for bookshelves
and coffee tables.

the weather is unkind,
but kismet likes me just fine.

It hurts.
And it is hard.

No one tells ya.
Travels tell me to.

Be a poet
You stupid idiot.

No one reads me shit.
Anyway.

Ant Hills

This is part two of something.
Skank danced last night.
I got some time with my Achilles.
On SE Division Street.
Leaving Ladd's Addition.
To new work level.
Overhearing the cursing feet.
Gutter punks utter something.
Then they give me the finger.
I found a baseball at the bus stop.
Along the river.
I sell some books.
Books that I wrote.
Put anxiety behind me.
Eventually play catch with said gutter
punks.

Skateboarding and Books
and Her and Her and Her

It's good to have passions,
Still the wind when it blows;
I can literally hear
when it gets ghost cold.

Hold on, my friend Steve,
to warm youth
for as long as your fingers
have bones inside them.

Has love read you to sleep
with page 32,
sticking to the curb
appealing to light.

Be me and be me twice,
lies and all
with chocolate chips
and her face's lips.

Catch your breath
while having your breath taken away;
your window shakes,
fall for legs that left you for dead.

In the end,
it is just the end
and coyotes will eat your corpse
but not your loves or the books you've read.

Vane

as in spire,
telling time which way is west,
I sit on a roof,
pointing out the horizon
for folks who can't seem to see it.

definition
left for dead,
 a feather fastened to the shaft near the nock
of an arrow.

mistakes make us infinite.
 I was a windmill once.

Names

Nick Del'Angelo.
Keren Amihud.
Marc Carusiello.

*Plus films
and fucks,
forever
and luck.*

Where do you see yourself
In the memories of others?
Just a name or nothing.
More, I heard it.

Digest Days

Late to early.
Night to morning.
Egg McMuffin.
Re-employment meeting.
Saw Danny Supa near Varick Street.

He was eating ice cream or pizza while
standing on his skateboard.

Took the train back uptown.
Saw a dead homeless lady.
Saw Natalie Portman walk by me.
She is probably in town for Rosh Hashanah.

Regretfully ate a Hot Pocket.
Watched part of Toy Story.
Late into work at the flower shop.
Read Agatha Christie on the bus.

Do your feet hurt?

Maria, I am in love with you from a distance

skateboard in short shorts,
you can draw it in and draw it back.
we probably met at a party
many years ago and said nothing.

instagram nights
turn into ceiling fans,
how deep is this whole hole?
I can ollie over you.

probably gonna go
jerk off twice in a row
and picture your tattoos
but also dinner scrumps.

we both know Brian Anderson
and I can only heel flip,
but the Saturday is this
and you are fine gone and gorgeous.

Poem

I am dumb.

But I Am The Only One Who Has My Name

Aside from that other Ryan Buynak
in Los Angeles,
I am my name, more so than ever before.

He didn't enter contests
at Badlands Skatepark
in Altamonte Springs, Florida,
placing 23rd.

And he didn't go to Spitvalves shows
at BT Grinders.

It's Been A Long Twelve Months

Please don't forget me.
Your name is San Francisco Lantern.
I was borne for this.
Yet love broke my ribs.

I see you at the gastro pub.
Once in a while.
And you should know.
That longboarding isn't skateboarding
And barista-ing isn't bartending.

Beautiful fool, you.
Be forever.
In pages like this.
Burned at the edges.
Of years gone by.

Maybe I will meet you in Portland.
Or the middle.
Perhaps.
If the fortunes feel better.
By never nights.

Add Punk Rocker to This

In your heart,
there are heaps of stuff,
growing wild
when you grow old.

Doesn't matter
if you don't rich it like a river,
it will eat you to the grave
like the smells of wishes.

My patchwork tattoos
tell a story,
even the Ghostbusters one on my butt,
and I just copied my punk rock heroes.

This Seems Like a Good Stopping Place

right after good news
mixed with bad news
and a bad pedicure,
the sun disappears.

page 82.
or 84.
is better than 32.
Page 260/267.

Warm Rolling Rocks
for Breakfast!

a TV that,
for some stranger,
unknown reason,
won't turn off.

unless you unplug it
and then,
for some strange
unknown reason
it takes ten days
to turn back on.

the fish died in August
of that year.

we call it last year.
oh.

booking the LA gig

my fingers, goddamn.
this song, goddamn.
the future, confused by the wind.
today, remaining love.

I have seen so much.
joy, pain, bullshit, regret.
I only have advice.
But you know your way.

can't catch me with flower port shine.
but if you choose to be a murderous bird.
remember my legs and heart.
because they finish for your evil in time.

doesn't matter where we are.
or what your small hands shake.
before I hope, after mine.
lesson sharp than my music and my lonely
poems, think of nothing else.

does this shit still work?

I got a thing in my heart,
some burning,
but no one knows
unless they see smoke.

blogs are firewood,
and words are fireworks,
ready to blow up
with violent eyes.

get purple
because weapons
are no hearts
and now hearts are sonic booms.

from front yard vacancies,
we can see the sea
and give up
on it all.

none of this works
in ghost spirit spit ball nonsense,
let the guitar and the keyboard meat
meet us on the other side of the blvd.

if you let me go back in time

to be a better GIF,
I will give you every thing
the ceiling has to offer.

All Before Noonish

10 cups of coffee,
some whiskey,
two wishes,
a blowjob from my neighbor,
three songs by The Killers,
a skate slam on 3rd ave,
and a stop-and-chat
with an ex-girlfriend.

Wow,
I got soul,
but this is ridiculous,
and poems are stupid,
especially these days
when nothing much matters
outside the terrible news.

At 12:01pm,
it feels like the day has
lived a thousand lives,
and with all these things
that I have done,
I feel like I could die
at lunch, drowning
in a sandwich with too much mayo.

Lauren and Jason and Me

skipped the Sunday part
of the poetry fest
and had a mellow skate day
with the birthday boy.

We met his lady
at Max Fish
for a dinner drink,
joining the rims of our pint glasses.

Lauren asked me
if I was seeing anyone,
and I laughed,
and then she asked if I was staying
in New York.

I didn't answer,
not to be rude,
but I just didn't know;
every time I think it's for good, something
else pulls me away.

Jason leaned over my shoulder
to see who I was texting.

"Who is Frances, some girl you met on the
subway?"
Yes, a beautiful reader.

They left around midnight,
heading to their home in Queens.
I stayed for another round,
and Bumbled for a few pretty legs between
which to sleep.

Dave Just Dave

the brown dog is asleep
in the living room,
his pitbull eyelids fluttering
as he dreams of puppy things.

this place is lovely like the 90s,
but smells like cigarettes
from the last tenants,
and we even ripped out the carpet
to put in a skate ramp
that leads to the kitchen,
where the beer is for breakfast.

sleeping here is both
anxious and exciting,
where as nights are full
of punk rock parties,
days are spent trying to figure out
her name and where I put my keys,
but it doesn't matter because
the door is never locked.

I write poetry in the backyard
while Dave is at work, where
he sells white people bonds,
but really can't describe what

he does to me or anyone else.

I feel like I am in college again,
but learning more
and not feeling bad
about ditching class to get high
or chase skirts downtown,
or go surfing at sunrise,
and skateboarding at dawn.

on this particular night,
we all sit silent and watch tv,
flipping back and forth
from basketball to Bonanza
for some reason,
and I only know two of the
ten people here.

the brown dog wakes up
and knocks over my beer,
no one moves or cares
as the now-exposed concrete floods,
and the dog barks at bats
fluttering their wings in the backyard.

Evening Rollerskates
(Freaking Farms)

Once upon a time,
back in time,
between two farms,
there was a little girl
who just wanted to rollerskate,
but being stuck in a rural world of dirt
didn't allow her the luxury
of 'shoes with wheels'.

She asked her Father the farmer
for Christmas, he said no.
She asked her Mother the milkmaid
for her fourteenth birthday, Mother said no.

After a year of saving her nasty nickels
and damned dimes, she finally had enough
to buy herself some rollerskates,
so she went to town
and bought herself rollerskates,
but after she purchased them,
as she was walking back from town,
she realized she was miles
from any concrete.

Her Father the farmer was strict,
her mother the milkmaid was drunk and
disapproving.
"No man will marry a girl who rollerskates,"
Mother would scream.

The girl attempted to ride the skates in the
gravel dirt driveway
one day when her folks were away
buying cattle steed,
but she fell in the first minute
and skinned her knee.
"Freaking farms," she screamed.

Just when she was about to give up
and sell her skates to the river,
she had an ingenious idea.

That night she put her nightgown
over her dungarees,
and pretended to sleep until
she heard both her parents
snoring like bears and boars.
She snuck out of the house with her
rollerskates in hand.
She went to the older barn
on the east end of the property

where she proceeded to move everything
from the top floor.
It was wood and warped,
but once the hay was gone
and the rats were chased away,
the girl had a nice little circle in which to
skate the night away.

Once she got her footing,
she spun and spun for hours
in veritable silence,
but her smile was as loud as lightning.

As the sun began to rise,
she threw the hay back to its pointless place
and hid her rollerskates under a donkey.
She snuck back into bed,
and smiled again, loudly,
thinking about her special rollerskating
hiding place.

It was hers and only hers.

the genuine night is always borrowed from us

the streets are soft at two.
my skate shoes hurt the concrete skin.

unless summer changes my name,
today makes tonight makes tomorrow
never the same.

sirens drive by with lights.
cops carry knives.
cigarettes are flicked off of fire escapes.
I dreamed I saw you in red suspenders.
I am a bartender.

tomorrow,
I will throw a rock through your window.

tonight,
I will fall asleep with a half-eaten ham
sandwich in my sheets.

wander 'round.
walk with legs and feet
and scar the streets
of the east.

something beyond me.
trash on the sidewalk,
stirs sweet talk
from drunk passers-by.

I am old newspapers,
swept from April into May.
Call out to no one.
Call out to me.
From somewhere across the breeze.

After all is said and done,
I feel the same.
Just another exiled king
of a thousand years of other people's nights,
with one scheme in mind.

mine, at least.
incomplete copper to the touch.
and in the green morning
I will carve your pineapple name into the
back of my seaward eyes...
as I walk home,
one step closer to next-year's first snow.

I'll get back to you someday
about tonight.

meretricious

tonight and tomorrow and the next day
and the day after that,
life is a kind of happy death paragraph,
powerful stuff.

this jacket was made in England,
it says,
and these boots in France.
this grey scarf was made
on Delaware Avenue.

it don't take long for the demons to come
visit me.

what, filled.
shitty poems.
honest, at least.
busted ankles and bloody nose.
it is very cold.
out.
always nothing.
textmessages,
sunny winter days,
the library on 96th street,
new music for new memories,

hopefully,
all unwanted soup.
always nothing.
dollar bills for the juke,
leftover Puerto Rican food.
talk of bar fights.
shoulders, mine.
talk of absentee women.
talk of better bars.
textmessages.

the condensation drips off my bottle
of Budweiser Light.
chicken pickles,
always nothing,
except little heart attacks
and funny sunsets.
weird wobbly tables, bullshit nights, spiders.
tomorrows.
Irish coffee, American taxes,
brave, still not bold.

Manicotti karate,
always nothing
in every direction.
Silence!
Gambling.
Double or nothing

on the Chicago Bears,
on true love.

The last Sunday of every Sunday,
powerful stuff:
zero afternoons, bang elbow skate, and
freezer-cold wakes
without much in the way of corpses.
what, filled.
shitty poetry.
mine, at least.
always nothing.
all I got.

This morning,
the shittiest weed at dawn,
fifteen degrees on the streets,
always nothing.
empty stomach growling in between beats of
my wayward heart.

Not going to Taiwan.
Studying German literature.
Now the Dandelion Rebellion
grows in the middle
of railroad tracks.

kay two seven, other stuff

pull me over.
park my truck.
kick me in the dick.

because I have been
burning memories lately
in forever fires
called giving up
for good or ill.

I just need something
for which to move on,
drive away, cycle,
say adios to the devil
and kick the shovel
which kicks the dirt.

Don't Shirk

over the turnstiles,
stealing the day,
out on my skateboard,
trying to settle down,
if I could settle up.

run from the heat,
rub one out on the street,
cigarettes and orgasms.
the night will be hungry
with gun snacks.

warriors don't warrior,
what did you expect?
I'll be in a cabin
in the woods when
you read this.

I wanna strange life,
and a strange love
with a hyphen in the middle,
out on tour,
missing fucking in New York.

my knuckles will never
be the same

after dreaming;
I can't believe
it is July 2020!

Be Young

Forever.

One of the Wonderful Weirdos

riding a motorcycle
in the rain,
sans helmet,
listening to Merle Haggard
on the headphones,
drowning out the
cartoons and the boxes,
while also eating a wet chili dog.

maybe I will take off my pants
at the next red light
to really turn some heads;
is it illegal to pilot a motorcycle
in only black Calvin Klein
boxer briefs?

with skateboard bungee-corded
to the bitch seat,
I gotta get there before lightning
and before Rory goes and wins,
before she disappears for good or ill,
and before I die
in glass and screams.

embarrassing strangers is fun,
especially black strangers

because they are a tougher audience in
minute passing.

the splash of orange in front of me
is not my fault, Kevin!

I ride north
and yell at the rumbling clouds,
and think about the Rumbler
and Harlem.
it's been a while since
I rumbled or made
love; fucking is different.

see you after the commercials,
after the storm,
after regret, after Rory and Tory.

stuff is sweet.
right, Kevin?

Nightcap Sunrise

there is,
in each of our
secret eyes,
day-in
and
day-out competition
to win
the battle of life.

my weapons include:
a skateboard,
drawing pens,
words,
love.

holding close,
old New York.

my weapons include:
basketball,
rivers,
cookies,
television meditation,
love.

holding close,

enjoyable regret.

we will all lose
this battle,
but ain't it fun
to fight?

you know I am right,
every tonight.

Mark Hill Poem

There are spiders in the toilet
and they make me afraid of love,
not like live lady bugs
and Mark Hill is on the come up.

Marty been feelin' weird,
like he gotta get outta here
and move to LA,
but I keeps tellin' him
that LA is lonesome,
and it makes you feel 18,
but illegal and uncool,
and it burns like Florida
with exponents and death
and Honda Civics.

But he says back to me
that that is exactly what he wants.

So I says to him that he needs
to conquer his Wal-Mart fears
and if he loses,
then he loses nada,
unlike freckles in Miami,
where love is still bullshit

to this day,
but leave with a warning of
Sunset BLVD, because
it will do the same.

I've been there and done that;
it treated me like shit in 2004,
but it gave me poetry,
and ultimately it gave me love,
and NYC.

So I says to him,
before having to get off the phone,
that he should do it.

Go be a DJ, I says,
and live on a boat
and make us all jealous.

Caves

One, two, three!
little Dorothies of water
lined up in the kitchen sink.

Obviously done by a wayward fork
with issues,
who got up and walked
out of here
with my finger skateboard,
without name,
turning back on me
through a window
somewhere in Brooklyn.

You never cease to amaze me, muse.

Cocaine is there, too,
at least yesterday, 'twas...

like me, like you, like Saturday lightning,
you goddamn Fork.

Unforgiving.
Life is unforgiving, too.

Badische of...duh,
and more words,
God is grossish...

at least to me.

I sigh, show my back,
the kitchen is a nightmare.

I listen to Tokyo Police Club
in better head phones
than before,
because of a stranger
who paid me to name them.

Tomorrow.

with seven exclamation points,
he will be a green apple,
and I am him.
The one with the point of view.

Unlike,
as the crow hears the news
from the mewed newspapers,
the dishes are done.

God is goodish, again.

I guess for the second time.
We are Love, in-fucking-deed.

Despondent

addiction is like that...

floorboards
and morning rain,
shaking in sheets now and then without
emotional wisdom
or a car to take me into the city.

break down the corridors.

yellow.
city birds.
thirteen and a half words.

vomit.
drink booze.
skateboard.
write (like this bullshit, prickling, coming).

happiness and jealousy
are things I haven't seen in a long year,
simultaneously simultaneous.

backwards.
humiliated.

tossed.
brother.

wish I was a transient slut.
money does buy happy shit.
wishing over draw bridges, too, dear.
call it one drink too many.

45 Days a Hero

I windowed left
and rivered right,
passing tigers
and chain gangs,
back in time.

on this night,
four years ago,
I was tending bar
in Union Square
when she texted me
a terrific defeat.

life changes in seconds,
often remembered as
massive moments when
memories are all we have.

and for the next 45 days,
I was her hero,
and love was real.

That was four years ago,
which is like high school
or college, and
my, how time flies

and love fades,
but it's okay,
I have archeological proof.

no one wants to hear folk songs anymore

I write asshole poems
made of whiskey midnights;
I have made a few mistakes
in my time.

after ten years
of tending bar,
it wasn't for me
anymore
in the eyes.

I am forever
in forever
or forever
with the devil
in the eyes of the inside.

just dance
in things called years
as they pierce your ears
with moments.

pay the rent
with happiness

and comb the trees,
enjoy the regrets.

knives in frying pans
and college literature talks,
but in the famous morning
I call shotgun to romance!

pass the hearts
and learn some things,
shake like dandelion
while asking for names.

need the days
like the nights need space
and disappear
without a trace.

get dumb in print,
a little bit of life is stuck in my teeth,
and poetry is what I eat,
so give me your fingers for...

igualmente

we all have boogers
and only some of us are
good at spelling.

I not good at math.
and
I really don't know how the stock market
works.

dumb smart kids,
but...

gosh darn it all.

I kicked a guy out my bar
a month ago
because he kept talking shit about the
Orlando Magic.

inre: we all have limits/pride.

the digger is nicked and forlorn for
casualties over pop culture lunch for two for
fifty dollars and a wallet full of wine.
over and out.

I love forever it.

now I figure I'd go north or west or on a
date.

Long Ago
aka
What I Want to Fuck Up

I should've listen to you,
but I was deep in chemical courage.

My Thesis/Your Prompt

For years, yawns and yelps,
 I did things…
         and they still stick with me.

Think about the things that stick with you,
no matter how silly.

Mix CD, 86th Street Crosstown Bus

1. *Bushwick Blues* by **Delta Spirit**
2. *Neighborhood #2 (Laika)* by **Arcade Fire**
3. *Wolf Like Me* by **TV on the Radio**
4. *Hospital Beds* by **Cold War Kids**
5. *The Great Escape* by **We Are Scientists**
6. *Centennial* by **Tokyo Police Club**

Comedy, Worry
& Peanut Butter Desks

I'll be honest,
I don't remember one bit about it.
I was all hopped up on cocaine back then
that I took anything I could get
in terms of women and want.

Can't say much for 95th Street,
because I don't rightly know
Where I lived was actually a place
and not an imagined Puerto Rican boneyard
where bartenders went to parish after shifts,
after love.

But in hindsight, which is not 20/20,
my scars will itch when the weather
is just right for drinking rain on some
anniversary of some dead relationship
or some burned down restaurant.

I don't know, who am I?
Just some question mark kid
from the ghetto who has seen some shit
and incrementally keeps getting better
at figuring out fuckups and misfortunes.

In the end, we are all just dumb dumbs,
who waste our youth on booze and love,
and love and booze and who's who's
of more wasted youth left where
the sun don't shine.

So, don't follow me, kids, because
my mistakes made me and your mistakes
need to make you,
for your death depends on it,
and mine now only depends on time,
plus a little petrichor, panic, and planning.

I'm a Man with a Southern Secret

The devil tastes ya.
When a hummingbird dies in flight.
But remember to hold out.
For what's right.
Because we are all gonna die.
At the right time.

Poem

I will always know tea
and how to make a Perfect Manhattan.
Equal parts sweet and dry vermouth.

I will always see stairs
and ollie them in my mind.

I will always write hard about soft love
left in the kitchen after a drunken night
of howling at the moon like crazy coyotes
in Central Park.

Ryan Buynak is a volunteer poet…meaning he loves this shit so much that he would do it any time, anywhere, for free.

He is a hugger yet a fighter. He was a bartender (for 15 years), he will always be a skateboarder (no matter how much he kicks and pushes), and he was born to be a writer (just look at his hands).

This book was started hard in the rumbling sprang of 2009, in the middle of it all (coyotes and death), but it spans a lifetime of learning, love, weird lessons and mistakes. It is about youth and youngmanhood.

Mr. Buynak doesn't need your forgiveness; all he needs is laughter.

He owns 7 and a half hidden hatchets.

95486420R00183

Made in the USA
Columbia, SC
12 May 2018